W9-AHV-248

The California
Gold Rush

Michael V. Uschan

WORLD ALMANAC® LIBRARY

To Barbara Roark, librarian extraordinaire

Please visit our web site at: www.worldalmanaclibrary.com
For a free color catalog describing World Almanac® Library's list of high-quality
books and multimedia programs, call 1-800-848-2928 (USA) or 1-800-387-3178
(Canada). World Almanac® Library's fax: (414) 332-3567.

Library of Congress Cataloging-in-Publication Data

Uschan, Michael V., 1948-
    The California Gold Rush / by Michael V. Uschan.
        p. cm. — (Landmark events in American history)
    Includes bibliographical references and index.
    ISBN 0-8368-5374-1 (lib. bdg.)
    ISBN 0-8368-5402-0 (softcover)
    1. California—Gold discoveries—Juvenile literature. 2. Frontier and pioneer
life—California—Juvenile literature. 3. California—History—1846-1850—
Juvenile literature. [1. California—Gold discoveries. 2. Gold and gold mining—
California—History—19th century. 3. Frontier and pioneer life—California.
4. California—History—1846-1850.] I. Title. II. Series.
    F865.U83   2003
    979.4'04—dc21   2002036021

First published in 2003 by
World Almanac® Library
330 West Olive Street, Suite 100
Milwaukee, WI 53212 USA

Copyright © 2003 by World Almanac® Library.

Produced by Discovery Books
Editor: Sabrina Crewe
Designer and page production: Sabine Beaupré
Photo researcher: Sabrina Crewe
Maps and diagrams: Stefan Chabluk
World Almanac® Library editorial direction: Mark J. Sachner
World Almanac® Library art direction: Tammy Gruenewald
World Almanac® Library production: Jessica Yanke

Photo credits: Bancroft Library, University of California: p. 25; California History Room,
California State Library: pp. 23, 24, 26; Corbis: cover, pp. 4, 5, 14, 16, 17, 18, 18, 20,
27, 28, 29, 32, 33, 34, 41, 42; Fort Ross Historical State Park: p. 8; Little Bighorn
Battlefield National Monument: p. 40; North Wind Picture Archives: pp. 6, 7, 9, 10, 12,
13, 15, 21, 22, 30, 31, 35, 36, 37, 38, 39.

Printed in the United States of America

1 2 3 4 5 6 7 8 9 07 06 05 04 03

Contents

Introduction

During the Gold Rush, gold hunters would rush off to California, convinced they would strike it rich. Newspaper and magazine cartoons of the time, such as this one, made fun of people with gold fever.

An Attack of Gold Fever

"I looked on for a moment; a frenzy seized my soul; unbidden my legs performed some entirely new movements of Polka steps—I took several. . . . I was soon in the street in search of necessary [mining equipment]; piles of gold rose up before me at every step; castles of marble, dazzling the eye with their rich appliances; thousands of slaves, bowing to my beck and call, were among the fancies of my fevered imagination. In short, I had a very violent attack of the Gold Fever."

James H. Carson of Monterey, California, recalling his emotions on seeing a sack of gold nuggets, 1848

Gold Fever

Throughout history, the desire to possess gold has made people greedy. This greed is known as "gold fever," and it sparked an important event in American history when gold was discovered in California.

Discovery in California

On January 24, 1848, James W. Marshall found small pieces of the glittering metal in the American River near present-day Coloma. When news of Marshall's startling find became known, the California Gold Rush began. The quest for gold caused a huge **migration** that changed the nation forever.

Rush For Riches

In just four years, almost 250,000 miners, farmers, businessmen, and others arrived to settle in California. In 1850, as a result, what had been a remote **frontier** area became the nation's thirty-first state.

In future years, the continued lure of gold in other areas of the West helped bring more people to create new western states such as Nevada, Utah, and Colorado. Marshall's accidental discovery had the consequence of speeding up the process of westward expansion, by which settlers—nearly all of them white people—came to inhabit a vast area from the Atlantic to the Pacific Ocean.

The Value of Gold

Gold is valuable because, compared to non-precious metals, it is rare. Its value has to do with its qualities, too: not only is gold beautiful, but it is the easiest metal to work with. It can be hammered into slivers thinner than paper or shaped into jewelry and coins. It has a deep, rich, yellow color that can be polished to a dazzling brilliance; and it doesn't rust.

Traditionally, gold has often been used as a unit of **currency**. Since it has value worldwide, unlike the paper currency of a particular country, gold was used for international transactions. In the days of the Gold Rush, wealth and the value of money used to be based on how much gold a nation owned. This is not true today, however, because the value of money is no longer simply based on solid things such as gold or land.

Chapter 1

California under Many Flags

Nearly all California Indians lived by hunting and gathering food because, in most areas, there were good supplies of wild foods. This Native hunter is from the Sierra Nevada region, where gold was discovered.

Native Californians

The first inhabitants of California probably arrived in the region about 15,000 years ago. In the period before the first Europeans settled in California, an estimated 300,000 Native American people lived there in more than 100 different groups.

The people of different groups had diverse ways of life that depended on their environment. Most lived in fertile regions, close to the abundant Pacific Ocean. Others lived in desert or mountain regions where food supplies were less plentiful.

Spanish Conquest

In 1542, Juan Rodríguez Cabrillo became the first European to visit California. Sixty years later, in 1602, Sebastian Vizcaíno sailed along its coast. He gave names to places that still exist today, such as San Diego and Santa Barbara. The Spanish claimed California as a **colony**. They called the area Alta—meaning "higher"—California because it was north of Baja—or "lower"—California, which is the Baja Peninsula that is now part of Mexico.

The Spanish did not settle in Alta California until 1769, when a Spanish colonial official, José de Gálvez, sent an expedition there. It included a Catholic priest, Junípero Serra. With the help of soldiers, Serra established a string of twenty-one **missions** that became centers for farming and ranching. The missions relied on the Native population for labor. Even though the California Indians greatly outnumbered the Spanish, they were quickly overcome by

Wiping Out the Native Population

The mission system and the arrival of European diseases combined to devastate the Native people of California. By the 1840s, after less than a century of colonial occupation, a population that had flourished for thousands of years was halved. By 1900, after thousands of settlers had arrived during the migration started by the Gold Rush, fewer than sixteen thousand Native Americans lived in California. Many of them lived on reservations.

the invaders' guns and cannons. Many Native Americans fled the newcomers, but thousands were forced into labor at the missions.

In the 1700s and early 1800s, Spain suffered little competition for California's rich **natural resources**, which included harbors for ocean-going ships, farmland, forests, and many types of animals and fish. There were only a few English ships that stopped to trade and a handful of Russian fur hunters.

Spanish and Mexican control of California lasted for nearly one hundred years, during which time settlers founded first missions and then large ranches. This is a Californian ranch during the 1800s, before the arrival of Americans.

The Russian Presence

For a short time, Russia competed with Spain in California. The Russians were interested in furs, especially valuable sea otter pelts. In August 1812, a party of Russians landed at Bodega Bay in northern California and established Fort Ross as a trading center. "Ross" is generally considered to be short for *Rossiya*, a name for Russia. The fort was built on the site of a Kashaya Indian village called Meteni.

Although successful at first, the Russian outpost later became unprofitable. In December 1841, the Russians sold the fort to Johann Augustus Sutter, who was starting his own business empire at the site of the present-day city of Sacramento.

Fort Ross in 1841.

Mexican California

By the early 1800s, Spain controlled a huge empire in North and South America. Because Spain governed its colonies brutally, however, people in countries it ruled began to fight for their independence. In 1821, people living in Mexico revolted against Spain. They won their freedom and established the **Republic** of Mexico. This included Alta California, where Spanish-speaking residents called themselves "*Californios*." There were only about three thousand Californios.

Manifest Destiny

The first U.S. citizen to reach this new Mexican **province** was Jebediah Smith, a legendary **trapper** and mountain man who explored the West. He visited California in 1826, but it was not until 1841 that the first wagon train of U.S. settlers from Missouri traveled along what became known as the California Trail. They were no doubt lured to California by glowing reports from previous visitors, such as one mountain man who claimed it was "a perfect paradise, a perpetual spring."

These settlers were the first of tens of thousands of pioneers who would realize the American belief in **Manifest** Destiny. This was the conviction that Americans should rule the entire continent from the Atlantic to the Pacific Ocean. It was this unshakable conviction that would soon cause war between the United States and Mexico.

> **Multiplying Millions**
>
> "It is our Manifest Destiny to overspread the continent allotted by Providence for the free development of our yearly multiplying millions. . . . Texas is now ours [and] California will, probably, next fall away from [Mexican control]."
>
> *John L. O'Sullivan,* United States Magazine and Democratic Review, *1845*

Settlers rest on the Plains on their way to California. In spite of the common image of wagon trains being attacked by Indians, the Plains people more often helped white travelers by acting as guides and trading animals and food.

The flag used in the Bear Flag Revolt was created by William Todd, a nephew of future president Abraham Lincoln. The revolt lives on in the California state flag, which also depicts a bear.

The Mexican War

Mexico and the United States had been on hostile terms since Americans living in the Mexican province of Texas revolted in 1836 and established the Republic of Texas. In 1845, the United States was trying to resolve differences with Mexico over the Mexican border with Texas, which had become a state that year. During negotiations, the United States also sought to buy California, an area it greatly desired, for $40 million. But Mexico refused the offer, and negotiations broke down. When Mexican soldiers attacked a U.S. force in Texas on April 25, 1846, President James K. Polk asked Congress to declare war.

The Bear Flag Republic

Congress declared war on Mexico on May 13, 1846. It did not take long for the news to reach California, where about two thousand American settlers lived under Spanish rule. A small band of about thirty Americans seized the city of Sonoma in California. On June 10, 1846, they proudly proclaimed their independence and raised a flag bearing the image of a bear. The Americans declared the formation of a new "California Republic."

The Bear Flag Revolt, as it was called, did not last long. On July 9, when U.S. naval forces arrived to occupy San Francisco and Sonoma, Commodore John D. Sloat proclaimed that "henceforward California will be a portion of the United States." The Bear Flag was thus replaced by the U.S. flag.

The Mexican War did not bring much fighting to the sparsely settled California, and hostilities there ended in January 1847, when Mexican official Andres Pico surrendered to Lieutenant John C. Frémont.

The United States Acquires California

The Mexican War ground to a halt at the end of 1847 and formally ended in May 1848, when both Mexico and the United States had approved the **Treaty** of Guadalupe Hidalgo. The treaty gave the United States more than 525,000 square miles (1,360,000 square kilometers) of land. This included the future states of California, Nevada, and Utah, most of Arizona and New Mexico, and parts of Colorado and Wyoming. In 1850, California became a state.

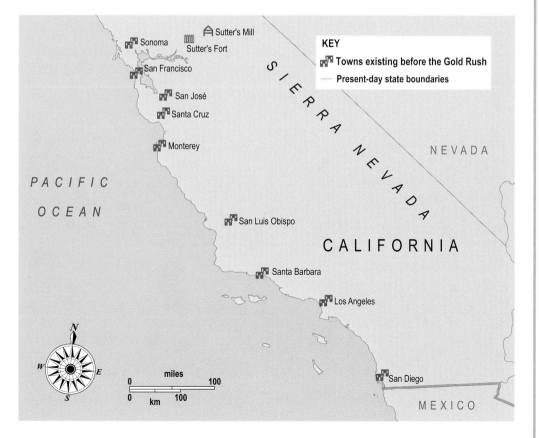

Before the Gold Rush, there were just a few towns in California. This map shows those settlements and the site of Sutter's Mill, where gold was found.

11

Chapter 2

The Discovery at Sutter's Mill

New Helvetia

Johann Augustus Sutter settled in California in 1839, having arrived in America a few years earlier with a dream of becoming rich. California was then a Mexican province. Sutter convinced Mexican officials to grant him 50,000 acres (20,000 hectares) of land located at the junction of the American River and the Sacramento River.

Sutter called his settlement New Helvetia ("Helvetia" is another name for his homeland, Switzerland), but it was known as Sutter's Fort because of the tall walls that protected it. In a few years, Sutter owned wheat farms, a flour mill, more than 12,000 cattle and 10,000 sheep, and a shipping line that carried passengers and freight on the Sacramento River to San Francisco.

New Helvetia, or Sutter's Fort, became a center for trading and settlement in the 1840s. Today it is the site of Sacramento, the capital of California.

Johann Augustus Sutter (1803—1880)

Johann Augustus Sutter was born in Germany to a Swiss family. He came to North America in 1834 after failing at various businesses in Switzerland. (Sutter left behind his wife and children but later brought them to America.) After a long journey that took him through parts of the southwest, Canada, Alaska, and even Hawaii, Sutter settled in California. He borrowed money to start his businesses after acquiring land grants from Mexico.

Sutter's dream of becoming rich turned into a nightmare when gold was discovered. Gold seekers destroyed his farms, fields, and stores and stole his livestock. Sutter failed to become rich by finding gold himself. Said Sutter: "By this sudden discovery of the gold, all my great plans were destroyed." Sutter was so bitter that in 1865 he left California and moved to Pennsylvania.

Gold

In August 1847, Sutter and James Marshall, a carpenter, went into partnership to build a **sawmill**. The mill site was about 45 miles (72 kilometers) northeast of Sutter's Fort in the small mountain valley of Coloma, originally Cullumah, a Native American name that means "beautiful view." The mill, known as Sutter's Mill, was on the south fork of the American River, and the river's current was used to power the big saws that cut trees into lumber.

The sawmill was completed in December. On the morning of January 24, 1848, Marshall was inspecting the operation of the new mill. Noticing something shiny in the river, Marshall picked up a gold-colored pebble. "Hey, boys," said Marshall to his workers, "by God, I believe I have found a gold mine."

Something Shining

"It was a clear cold morning; I shall never forget that morning. As I was taking my usual walk [by the mill] my eye was caught by a glimpse of something shining. There was about a foot of water running there. I reached my hand down and picked it up; it made my heart thump, for I felt certain it was gold. The piece was about half the size and of the shape of a pea. Then I saw another piece in the water. After taking it out I sat down and began to think right hard. When I returned to our cabin for breakfast I showed the two pieces to my men. They were all a good deal excited, and had they not thought that the gold only existed in small quantities they would have abandoned everything and left me to finish the job alone."

James W. Marshall

James Marshall never made a fortune from his gold discovery. He failed in several mining ventures and was so poor by 1872 that the state of California granted him a pension. He died in 1885 and was buried near Sutter's Mill.

On January 28, Marshall rode to Sutter's Fort to show his partner what he had found. Sutter realized the gold could make him rich. Sutter did not own the land the mill was on, but **leased** it—in exchange for clothing and food—from the Yalesummi people who lived there. In spite of this, Sutter thought the rights to the gold would be his.

The News Gets Out

By mid-March 1848, accounts of the discovery had spread throughout California. Most Californians were not very excited. Gold had been found several times before—long ago by Spanish missionaries and recently at Placerita Canyon. Because nobody ever found enough to become rich, however, people did not pay much attention.

This changed when the Gold Rush got a huge boost from Sam Brannan, a San Francisco businessman. When Brannan visited Sutter's Mill and realized the gold **strike** was a large one, he decided to make money by selling supplies to miners. He bought shovels, picks, metal pans, and other things that people needed to hunt gold. He then opened a store at Coloma.

Next, in early May, Brannan ran down the streets of San Francisco—then a small town of only a few hundred people—shouting loudly, "Gold! Gold! Gold from the American River!" As people gathered around, Brannan showed them gold nuggets. The effect of Brannan's announcement was immediate. Many people jumped on horses and headed for Sutter's Mill. The California Gold Rush was underway.

Sam Brannan of San Francisco quickly figured out something that would be realized by many others as the Gold Rush progressed. The most reliable way to make money was not to hunt for gold, but to sell mining equipment and other necessities to the hordes of eager gold seekers.

Gold Mine Found

"GOLD MINE FOUND—In the newly made raceway of the saw-mill recently erected by Captain Sutter, on the American [River], gold has been found in considerable quantities. One person brought thirty dollars worth to New Helvetia, gathered there in a short time. California, no doubt, is rich in mineral wealth."

The Californian *newspaper, with the first story about the gold discovery,*
San Francisco, March 15, 1848

This is a replica of the sawmill built by Marshall's men in Coloma. The replica stands at the same site of the original, in what is now Marshall Gold Discovery Historic Park.

The Gold Rush Picks Up Speed

Most gold miners in 1848 were from California, Oregon, and other nearby areas. San Francisco and other California cities became deserted overnight. Farmers, store-keepers, and even doctors and ministers joined the mad dash for gold. On May 29, 1848, the *Californian*, the San Francisco news-paper that first reported the strike, announced it was going out of business because everybody had left town to hunt for gold.

Peaceful, beautiful Coloma Valley was overrun with gold seek-ers. They did not stop there. The Mother **Lode**, a belt of gold-bearing rock, stretched through the Sierra

Vast Deposits

"The discovery of these vast **deposits** of gold has entirely changed the character of Upper California. Its people, before engaged in cultivating their small parcels of ground and guarding their herds of cattle and horses, have all gone to the mines, or are on their way thither; laborers of every trade have left their work benches, and tradesmen their shops; sailors desert their ships as fast as they arrive on the coast. Many desertions, too, have taken place from the [U.S. military] garrisons within the influence of the mines."

Colonel Richard B. Mason, military governor of California, in a report sent to Washington, D.C., August 17, 1848

Nevada range of mountains for about 100 miles (160 km). The hunt for riches soon spread to the Feather River above Sacramento, to Downieville on the Yuba River, and to the San Joaquin River near the modern-day cities of Fresno and Merced. Miners found gold everywhere.

A Government Report

In May 1848, several hundred men were searching for gold; by the middle of the summer there were about 4,000, and by the end of the year between 8,000 and 10,000. The California Gold Rush was still small in 1848. This was soon to change, when California's military governor, Colonel Richard Mason, reported the extent of the find to the United States government. The news spread first through the United States and then around the world.

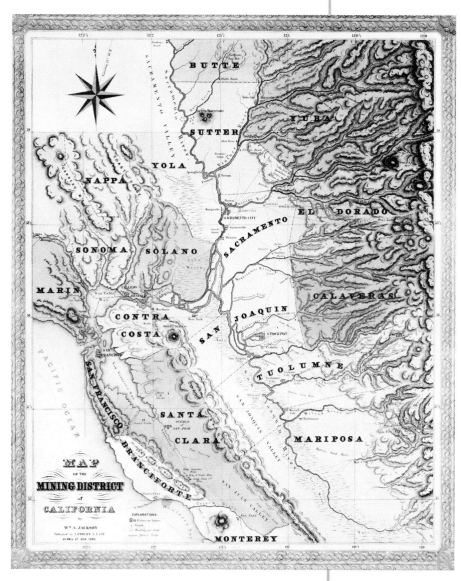

This map of California's mining region was drawn in 1851. The gold-producing areas stretched from north of Sutter's Mill to Mariposa in the south.

A Sordid Cry

"The whole country from San Francisco to Los Angeles and from the seashore to the [mountains] resounds to the sordid cry of gold! gold! GOLD!"

The Californian *newspaper, San Francisco, May 1848*

Chapter 3

The Forty-Niners

President James Polk's words caused a huge rush of Americans across the continent to California. Polk was a firm believer in Manifest Destiny. Many historians believe he had wanted war with Mexico in 1846 as an excuse to seize more territory, including California, for American settlement.

The President Spreads the Word

On December 5, 1848, following Mason's report, President James K. Polk confirmed the discovery of gold in a speech to Congress. Polk proclaimed, "The accounts of the abundance of gold in that territory are of such an extraordinary character as would scarcely command belief were they not corroborated by authentic reports of officers in the public service."

Polk's words made front-page headlines in newspapers across North America and then on other continents. Gold fever soon found its way to most corners of the world.

Untold Wealth

"The California gold fever is approaching its crisis. Thither is now setting a tide that will not cease its flow until . . . untold wealth is amassed. . . . The ground [in California] is represented to be one vast gold mine. Gold is picked up in pure lumps."

Hartford Daily Courant, *Connecticut,*
December 6, 1848

The Forty-Niners

In the decade before gold was discovered, only 2,700 people had moved to California. In 1849, some 90,000 newcomers arrived, even though the trip was difficult and filled with a host of dangers. They became known as "forty-niners," a term that also refers to those who joined the Gold Rush later.

It is hard to believe today that tens of thousands of people would leave their jobs, abandon their homes, and head for far-off gold fields as soon as they heard the news. But for most forty-niners, the reason was simple: it was a chance to have a better life.

The note one miner sent to his wife explains why he abandoned his family: "Jane, I left you and them boys for no other reason than this to come here [California] to procure a littl property by the swet of my brow so that we could have a place of our own that I mite not be a dog for other people any long." Like thousands of others, he believed the only way he could ever become rich was to find gold.

How They Got There

Before 1849, most Americans could not have found California on a map. It was a long way, beyond the **United States Territories** that were yet to become states. No railroads connected the two halves of the continent.

There were two main forms of transportation westward, both of them difficult. Most gold seekers chose to walk or ride a horse or wagon. To get to California, they had to cross the Great Plains, a large stretch of North America not yet settled by non-Native Americans. The most popular route started in Independence, Missouri, and ended 2,000 miles (3,200 km) and six months later in California.

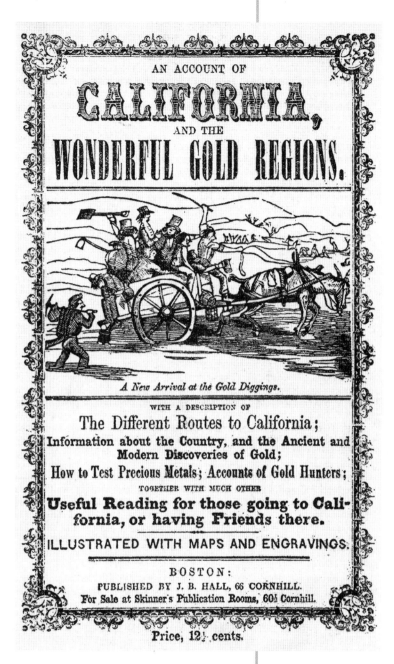

In this guide for forty-niners, the picture of the cart full of gold seekers shows the most common method of traveling west.

The Magnificent, Fast Sailing and favorite packet Ship,

JOSEPHINE,

BURTHEN 400 TONS, CAPT.

Built in the most *superb* manner of Live Oak, White Oak and Locust, for a New York and Liverpool Packet; thoroughly Copper-fastened and Coppered. She is a very fast sailer, having crossed the Atlantic from Liverpool to New-York in 14 days, the shortest passage ever made by a *Sailing Ship*. Has superior accommodations for Passengers, can take Gentlemen with their Ladies and families. Will probably reach 🖙 SAN FRANCISCO **THIRTY DAYS** ahead of any Ship sailing at the same time. Will sail about the

10th November Next.

For Freight or Passage apply to the subscriber,

RODNEY FRENCH,

New Bedford, October 15th. **No. 103 North Water Street. Rodman's Wharf**

Shipping lines encouraged the Gold Rush by advertising their services on posters. The journey around the tip of South America took many months.

Some forty-niners traveled by sea, but this journey was also tough. It took ships almost half a year to sail around the tip of South America to California from the eastern United States. Conditions on board the ships were terrible. Passengers became seasick, food was almost inedible, and living quarters were cramped and dirty. The trip was more expensive than going overland, costing between $100 and $300. These prices seem low today, but they were very high at the time in relation to what people earned.

Other forty-niners sailed south only to Panama in Central America. From there, they traveled overland to catch a second ship that carried them to California. This journey was shorter by several months than going around the tip of South

Then and Now

The sums of money that miners received for gold they mined during the California Gold Rush—as well as the prices they paid for travel, food, and other things—seem very low today. During the Gold Rush era, however, men and women did not have much money to spend. Most workers earned only a few hundred dollars each year, sometimes less than $200.

There are different ways to compare the value of money in past eras to today. One way is to consider what something cost in the past and what it costs today. A general rule of thumb is that an item purchased for $1 in 1848 would cost $20 today. This method is not always accurate, but it gives us an idea of the value of money in the 1840s and 1850s. A different rule applies to gold prices, which are 25 times what they were then.

Hopeful gold seekers find fresh air on the deck of a ship bound for California. Down below were dark, crowded sleeping quarters.

America. This trip was even more expensive than the others, however, and it managed to combine the discomfort and dangers of both forms of transportation.

Seeing the Elephant

The forty-niners who took any of those routes were vulnerable to malaria, cholera, and other diseases that killed thousands of them. Those who went overland also risked encounters with outlaws or with Indians resistant to white presence. They could die of thirst in the desert, become trapped in mountain passes if it snowed, or lose their lives in accidents.

In the 1840s, elephants were considered strange, mysterious creatures because they did not exist in America and few Americans had seen one. "Seeing the elephant" became a boast for anyone who had seen many unusual things. The people who made their way to California, by whatever route, encountered so many adventures and saw so many strange sights that they could proudly claim that they had "seen the elephant." Every forty-niner, no matter how he or she got to California, had "seen the elephant."

Traveling to California

"Start at 4—travel till the sun gets high—camp till the heat is over. Then start again and travel till dark. . . . After the Upper Platte Ford, for over fifty miles [80 km], the water is poisonous. If you would avoid sickness, abandon its use."

The Emigrants' Guide to California, *1849*

Crossing Panama seemed a quick and practical way to go from east to west. The journey was packed with dangers, however, as travelers had to pass through dense jungle.

Many Nationalities

Although 80 percent of forty-niners were Americans, people from other countries joined them, including hundreds of Pacific Islanders from Hawaii. (Hawaii is now part of the United States, but it was a separate nation then.) The Hawaiians who came to look for gold were called "Kanakas"—*Kanaka* is a Hawaiian word for "man." This name lives on in California place names such as Kanaka Creek.

In 1853, a French-language newspaper in San Francisco estimated that 32,000 French miners had arrived. They were nick-named "Keskydees," a word that sounded like *"Qu'est-ce qu'il dit?"*, the French phrase for "What is he saying?" This was a frequent question from French miners who could not speak English.

African Americans in California

In the first three years of the Gold Rush, California's African-American population doubled to more than two thousand people. One newspaper story claimed that, after a ship docked in San Francisco in September 1848, a white man asked an African-

American man to help carry his luggage. The second man pulled a pouch from his pocket and said, "Do you think I'll stoop to lugging trunks when I can get this much in one day?" It contained the equivalent of $100 ($2,500 today) in gold dust.

Most African-American miners were free men. Although some were brought to California as slaves, many were able to buy their freedom with gold they mined. The standard price of freedom was about $2,000 ($40,000 today), paid by the slaves to their owners. Some slaves managed to free themselves and their family members.

Women Forty-Niners

The California Gold Rush was almost entirely male. The 1850 California **census** showed that more than 90 percent of the state's residents were men. Nine years later, men still made up 60 percent of California's population.

Two African-American miners are shown here with two white men in Spanish Flat, California, in about 1852. They may have been slaves working to buy their freedom. The men in front are using a device called a long tom to sieve gold out of gravel by running water through the trough.

The women who came to California, either with their husbands or alone, found opportunities they would never have had in the East. Most women did not prospect for gold, but many made money providing services to the male forty-niners. They cooked, did laundry and other services, and ran many small businesses.

One woman wrote to a friend back home of her new opportunities: "A smart woman can do very well in this country. It is the only country I ever was in where a woman received anything like a just compensation for work." Another woman, Margaret Frink, made a large fortune by cooking: "I have made about $18,000 ($360,000 today) worth of pies—about one third of this has been clear profit."

This photograph from about 1852 shows a group of miners by the American River. The woman in the picture was one of few in the California mining camps.

Levi Strauss (1829—1902)

Levi Strauss was born in Bavaria and came to the United States in 1847. He worked as a salesman, traveling the back roads of New York State selling dry goods in remote rural areas. In 1853, Strauss came to San Francisco to work with his sister and brother-in-law in a dry goods business. Strauss would load a wagon with supplies and visit miners in the gold fields to sell them many things they needed. It was this business that made him prosperous during the tail end of the California Gold Rush.

In the 1850s and 1860s, Strauss sold pants made of tough canvas that would not tear. It was not until 1872, however, that metal rivets were added to his work pants. This strengthening feature made them hugely popular with miners and other working people, and by 1880, Strauss's business was reporting sales of over $2 million a year. The blue jeans became fashionable in the 1940s and have remained so ever since. Eventually, Levi's became the most famous pants of all time.

Some gold seekers brought with them things they thought they would need in California. This cartoon, entitled "The Independent Gold Hunter," shows a man weighed down with all kinds of goods, including a cooking pot on his head.

This group of miners includes three Chinese men. The photograph was taken in about 1852 and is one of the earliest known photographs of Chinese miners.

The Arrival of the Chinese

One of the largest groups of miners came the farthest, from China. In the 1840s and 1850s, ships sailed back and forth regularly from California to China, taking goods between the two continents. When the Chinese heard about the gold strike, thousands of them decided to go to the gold fields. Like everyone else, they hoped to become rich in America, which became known in China as Gam Saan, or "Gold Mountain."

It was the first time large numbers of Asians had emigrated to North America. The influx of so many Chinese had an effect on the continent's ethnic makeup. Until 1849, **immigration**—apart from the forced immigration of Africans in slavery—had been almost entirely European and had taken place in the East, not the West.

The Chinese who came to North America worked hard and performed many difficult and menial jobs that served the interests of white Americans. In spite of this, they were discriminated against for many decades.

The Chinese Community

When gold was discovered in 1848, only a handful of Chinese lived in California, but within a few years over twenty thousand Chinese people had immigrated there. The Chinese received a terrible reception. Most Americans in that era held prejudices about Chinese people. White people looked down on them because their skin color, language, and culture differed from their own.

A Chinese family in San Francisco's Chinatown in 1904.

United States officials created laws that made it hard for Chinese people to stay on U.S. land. In 1852, the California **legislature** passed the Foreign Miners' License Tax. Chinese and other foreign miners had to pay the state $20 ($400 today) a month to look for gold. This tax discriminated against foreigners, a group overwhelmingly made up of Chinese people. The tax was declared illegal in 1870.

The Chinese for many years were also prohibited from owning land. Despite such discrimination, many Chinese people established a community through hard work and perseverance. Today, because of Chinese immigration, California has the largest Asian population of any state.

Chapter 4.

The Gold Rush Years

California's Rapid Growth

In 1848, California was home to about 150,000 Native Americans and 14,000 people of European and Mexican descent, including about 2,000 Americans. By the end of 1860, because of the Gold Rush, its population had mushroomed to 380,000. California grew so quickly and its wealth became so significant that, in 1850, the territory was accepted as the thirty-first state of the United States.

Cities Appear

By the end of 1849, Sacramento, which grew up around Sutter's Fort, had 12,000 residents. And almost overnight, the wealth of the gold fields turned San Fancisco into one of the world's major cities. In 1847, San Francisco had only 450 residents, and in mid-1848 it became deserted as its residents rushed to Sutter's Mill. By late 1848, however, it was overflowing with 2,000 people. This number increased to over 20,000 within a year.

As the population of California exploded during the Gold Rush, it became hard to find somewhere to stay. The owner of this sheep pen charged four bits, or one dollar ($20 today), for a night's lodgings.

Until a couple of years before this photograph was taken in 1850, Montgomery Street in San Francisco had been the shoreline of Yerba Buena cove. The cove was completely filled to create more land. Streets filled with cable cars and wagons appeared where before there had been just water and a beach.

San Francisco

No California city grew more quickly during the Gold Rush than San Francisco, the small port town that had recently changed its name from Yerba Buena. In April 1849, it had only thirty or forty homes and a population of a few hundred. By September 1849, there were five hundred dwellings in San Francisco, and new homes were being built at the rate of several each day to accommodate its swelling population.

The demand for houses and the lack of workers to build them—almost everyone was looking for gold—was so great that houses were imported from China. Workers in that far-off country built homes and then cut them into pieces. The pieces were shipped to San Francisco, where they were then reassembled. The need for housing and business premises was so great that ships were brought into the harbor and leased as stores and hotels.

Miners set up tents outside of the central mining camps, close to where they were hunting for gold.

Mining Camps

Camps and makeshift towns sprang up around sites where gold was found. In the first ten years of the Gold Rush, more than five hundred known mining camps were established. The camps had strange, colorful names, such as Poker Flat, Devil's Retreat, Mad Mule Gulch, Gouge Eye, and Poverty Hill.

Mining camps were mostly primitive, with many businesses housed in tents or hastily constructed wooden shacks instead of wood or brick buildings. In these makeshift premises, businessmen and women made stores, saloons, laundries, restaurants, and hotels.

Miners regularly visited the camps to buy supplies and relax from their work. Their main entertainment was drinking and gambling. The camps were rough, lawless places filled with gamblers,

Staking a Claim

When gold seekers arrived in California, they couldn't just start mining for gold wherever they chose. First they had to stake a claim on a piece of land and register their claim with whatever authority was in charge of the district. Finding land worth claiming became increasingly difficult after the first months of the Gold Rush, because the most obvious and valuable sites had already been claimed. The first comers were the lucky ones, and some early claims yielded $400 ($10,000 today) worth of gold in a day, at least until the gold ran out.

The mining camps had a form of self-government to decide about the size of claims and the procedure for registering them. It could be difficult to defend a good claim, however, particularly for a miner who wasn't a white American. Some criminals tried, usually by force, to steal claims that were rich in gold. This was called claim jumping.

con artists, and criminals intent on getting money away from forty-niners by any method they could.

Life as a Forty-Niner

Most forty-niners lived in tents or shacks near the mining camps. Their life was one of poor living conditions and very hard work. In 1849 alone, about ten thousand people died due to illnesses caused by bad housing and food and lack of medicine.

Dry Diggings

The second big discovery of gold after Sutter's Mill came in an area south of the south fork of the American River, not far from Coloma. Gold was found there in June 1848, and within a week a thousand miners traveled there to seek their fortune.

Rascals with Soft Hands

"Hordes of pickpockets, robbers, thieves, and swindlers were mixed with men who had come with honest intentions. These rascals had lived all their lives by the sleight of hand and it was evident that they had not come to California with gold rings on their white, soft hands for the purpose of wielding the pick and pan in obtaining their wishes. Murders, theft and heavy robberies soon became the order of the day."

Forty-niner J. H. Carson

There were hardly any women in the rough surroundings of the mining camps. These miners danced with each other to provide entertainment in the evenings.

How the Forty-Niners Got Their Gold

The gold that the forty-niners found, if they were lucky, was in placers, or surface gold deposits in gravel and sand. The kind of mining they were doing was therefore called placer mining. The simplest form of placer mining is panning. Miners filled their iron pans with gravel and let water wash over it. Because gold is heavier than gravel, it would sink to the bottom of the pan while the gravel's sand and dirt were washed away. This was very tiring work. **Prospectors** had to stand in ice-cold water, bending over continuously while they let the water rush over their pans. Panning was slow; even a good miner could process only one hundred pans a day, which was a small amount of gravel.

Soon, miners began using devices known as long toms and sluices. Both were types of troughs with a sieving system that enabled them to process larger amounts of gravel much more quickly. Prospectors loaded gravel into the devices and then channeled water through them to get rid of the sand and dirt. This was much more efficient than panning.

The mining camp was named Dry Diggings because the river level fell in mid-summer. This meant the men had to carry the gravel they were digging for a distance of several hundred yards to water in order to wash the gold out of it.

A New Name

In January 1849, the camp got a new name. When some men tried to steal gold, they were captured and three of them were sentenced to be hanged. After that, Dry Diggings was called Hangtown.

As the mines continued to yield their riches, more people moved to Hangtown, many of them with families. Within a few years, the settlement drew more families as settlers interested in farming began to come to the area. Hangtown, despite its name, became a pleasant town with a church and a school. In 1854, the community's name changed again, to Placerville.

Although many mining camps vanished after a few months or a few years, others grew and developed the same way Dry Diggings did. They evolved from rough camps into communities that still exist today.

A Difficult Living

In 1848, miners panned gold worth nearly $10 million, or $250 million today. This figure quadrupled in 1849. People looking for easy riches were often disappointed, however. Mining was hard and sometimes dangerous, and there was no guarantee that miners would become rich.

Dry Diggings became Hangtown, and Hangtown became Placerville, all within a space of a few years. Unlike many mining camps, Placerville, seen here in 1900, survived and became an ordinary town.

A man is using hydraulic mining equipment to extract gold from the mountainside. Hydraulic mining became common when the easiest deposits of gold in the river and stream beds ran out.

The first to arrive did the best, and in 1848 many miners gathered hundreds or even thousands of dollars of gold each week. But as the gold fields became crowded and sites rich in gold became scarce, it became increasingly hard to make money. By 1853, individual miners were averaging $35 ($875 today) in earnings a week, an amount that continued to fall as the gold supply dwindled.

Large-Scale Mining

After the first few years, the thousands of hopeful miners had exhausted the placer deposits in river beds, which

Gold Production

The California Gold Rush produced hundreds of millions of dollars of gold. These are gold production figures in dollars for 1848 through 1856, the year considered to be the end of the California Gold Rush. The gold that was mined in that period was valued at $16 an ounce, a price set by the U.S. government. The price of gold today is almost $400 an ounce, or 25 times as much as then.

Year	Value of gold produced	Approximate value today
1848	$10 million	$250 million
1849	$40 million	$1 billion
1850	$50 million	$1.25 billion
1851	$60 million	$1.5 billion
1852	$81 million	$2 billion
1853	$65 million	$1.6 billion
1854	$60 million	$1.5 billion
1855	$55 million	$1.35 billion
1856	$56 million	$1.4 billion

were the easiest available sources of gold. Gold production remained high for decades, however, because of large-scale rather than individual mining techniques.

A more expensive form of placer mining, requiring machinery, was **hydraulic** mining. In this method, a high-pressure hose was used to direct a strong stream of water at the slopes and cliffs containing placer gold and flush it out of the gravel.

Underground Mining

When the surface deposits were running out, underground sources were explored. This meant drilling and digging deep **shafts** to mine gold embedded in rock underground. Shaft mining was expensive compared to placer mining, and only large companies or rich people could afford to mine gold in this way.

As it became more difficult for individuals to extract gold, many forty-niners left California broke and disheartened. One eastern newspaper commented: "Those who return home disappointed say that they have been humbugged [fooled] about the gold, when, in fact, they have humbugged themselves about the *work*."

Gold mining underground required a large investment. It was dangerous work for the miners who were employed to spend long days in the dark tunnels, chipping gold deposits out of the rock.

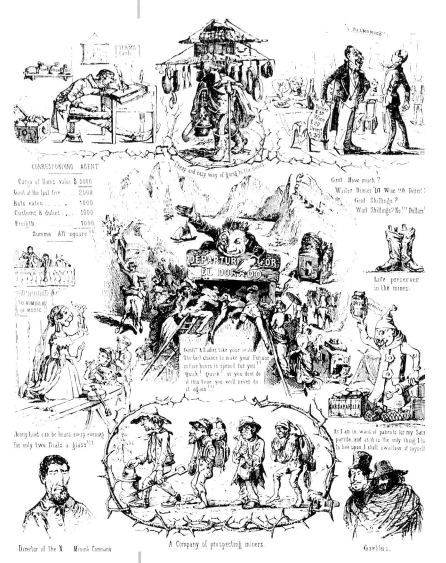

This cartoon, which ridicules the people in California during the Gold Rush, shows those who exploited the forty-niners in different ways.

High Prices

Mining, however, was not the only way to become rich during the Gold Rush. Sam Brannan made money selling supplies to miners from the first days in Coloma. Businessmen were able to sell supplies to miners at inflated, or very high, prices because the goods they sold were the only ones available. Sam Brannan, for instance, bought iron pans for 20 cents ($4 today) and sold them at mining sites for $8 to $16 ($160 to $320).

Prices were equally high for other items, such as food, that were scarce in camps. In the early days of the Gold Rush, a loaf of bread that would cost 5 cents ($1 today) in the East sold for 75 cents ($15) in San Francisco. Other high prices included 50 cents ($1) for an egg and $40 ($800) for a blanket. Small nails to anchor canvas tents sold for an unbelievable $192 ($3,840) a pound (0.45 kilogram).

Other Ways to Make Money

There were many other ways to earn a living during the Gold Rush years. People worked as teamsters driving wagons to get supplies to miners. Doctors and dentists cared for people in the mining camps. Blacksmiths shoed horses and mules and repaired mining equipment. People from every profession imaginable, including singers and actors, were able to move to California and make money.

Losers in the Gold Rush

Although many grew rich during the Gold Rush, the people who had lived in California the longest did not. When the Mexican War ended, the Treaty of Guadalupe Hidalgo declared that the United States would honor property rights of Mexicans in California. But when tens of thousands of Americans swarmed there after gold was discovered, U.S. officials took hundreds of ranches away from Mexican residents and gave the land to Americans.

Faring even worse were California's original inhabitants. In 1848, more than half the workers in the gold fields were Indians, but most were slaves who were forced to labor for others. Some Indians mined gold on their own. However, because Native Americans had few rights and were considered inferior, many were cheated out of the gold they did find.

The forty-niners, like the Spanish before them, brought diseases such as cholera and smallpox that killed many Native people. They also forced Indians off Native land and sometimes hunted them down and killed them.

Deliberate Extermination

"Extermination [of Native Americans] is no longer a question of time—since the time has arrived, the work has commenced, and let the first man that says treaty or peace be regarded as a traitor."

California newspaper the Yreka Herald, *advocating the killing of Indians, 1853*

The people who struck lucky could use their gold to trade for other things or take it to a bank and sell it. At this bank, gold dust brought in by miners is being weighed to assess its value.

Chapter 5

The Gold Rush Moves On

Moving to Other Areas

By 1854, the California Gold Rush was slowing down. The discovery of gold had sent thousands of people hurtling across the Great Plains to settle in California and other Pacific Coast areas. The result of this greed-driven migration was that both coasts of North America were populated by white Americans, while few were living in the vast open spaces in between.

Easterners seeking easy wealth continued to come west, however. Along with forty-niners who never struck it rich, they began prospecting elsewhere. They moved onto the Great Plains in the hope of riches, and they would swarm to any site where riches were discovered. White Americans began to settle vast areas that had previously been inhabited only by Native Americans.

Any word of new diggings led to a rush of hopeful miners such as these. After the California Gold Rush, prospectors appeared in many areas in and around the Rocky Mountains.

New Strikes

The first big strike after California was in Colorado in 1858, when both gold and silver were found near Pike's Peak. Once again, news of the discovery ignited a flood of miners and settlers. Thousands of people traveled there in covered wagons, some of which were painted with the phrase "Pike's Peak Or Bust!"

The Colorado find was the first of many discoveries in areas that eventually became U.S. states. These included what are now the states of Nevada, Arizona, Utah, and Montana.

Some of the richest mines were in Nevada, where—in the 1860s and 1870s—hundreds of millions of dollars in gold and silver were produced. Sandy Bowers became rich when, in 1859, he discovered silver and gold in a famous Nevada mine, the Comstock Lode. The former wagon driver built a big house and filled it with every luxury imaginable. "I've got money to throw at the birds," Bowers liked to boast.

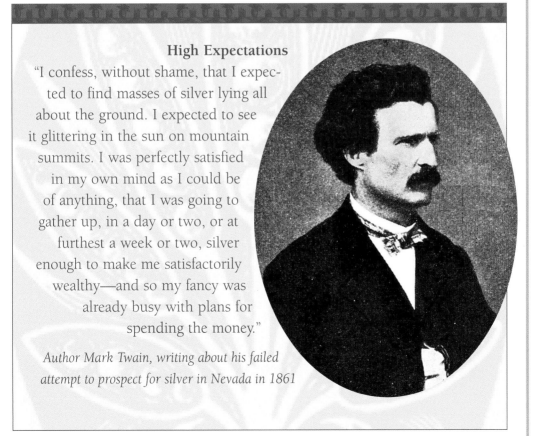

High Expectations

"I confess, without shame, that I expected to find masses of silver lying all about the ground. I expected to see it glittering in the sun on mountain summits. I was perfectly satisfied in my own mind as I could be of anything, that I was going to gather up, in a day or two, or at furthest a week or two, silver enough to make me satisfactorily wealthy—and so my fancy was already busy with plans for spending the money."

Author Mark Twain, writing about his failed attempt to prospect for silver in Nevada in 1861

Mark Twain in 1864, when he was working as a reporter in Virginia City, Nevada, after a failed attempt at mining.

Battles with Native Americans

Almost as soon as European colonists began arriving in North America, they began to fight with Native people over the land that would one day become the United States. And despite some victories in this long conflict, Native Americans steadily lost the long war for their homelands.

The California Gold Rush led to thousands of forty-niners crossing lands that had been home to Native American peoples for centuries. In the 1850s and 1860s, settlers began moving to these areas permanently, partly because of continued gold strikes. The result was warfare.

Once gold had been found in South Dakota, white Americans paid no heed to the Sioux Indians who had legal and traditional claims on the region. This mining operation in 1876 was right in the middle of Sioux homelands.

Little Bighorn

In 1874, Lieutenant Colonel George Armstrong Custer led an expedition into South Dakota's Black Hills. After Custer issued a report saying he had found gold, whites flooded onto land belonging to the Sioux. In June 1876, Custer's army attacked a large Indian camp near the Little Bighorn River. Custer and more than two hundred U.S. soldiers were killed in the resulting battle.

The Native victory in that battle sparked a final, all-out attempt by the United States to crush all Native American groups. In a little more than a decade, that goal was accomplished, and most Native people were confined to reservations within what had once been their homelands.

The Klondike

The last great gold strike was in 1896 in Alaska's Klondike region. Despite the cold and snow, so different from the searing heat of the desert where so much gold had been found, miners were tempted north by dreams of easy wealth.

The Gold Rush led to California quickly becoming a state, but the same thing did not happen in Alaska. The area was located far north of the United States, but it had been a U.S. possession since March 30, 1867, when the United States purchased it from Russia for $7.2 million. At the time, Secretary of State William H. Seward was ridiculed for buying such a bleak piece of real estate, and his purchase was nicknamed "Seward's Folly."

For three decades, Americans had largely ignored Alaska. But when gold was discovered, the inevitable happened. Miners came by the thousands, and Alaska, despite its harsh climate, began to develop cities and a small population that would continue growing. It was no longer a folly, but progress was slow. Alaska did not become the nation's forty-ninth state until 1959.

THE KLONDIKE NEWS

VOL. I.   DAWSON, N.W.T. APRIL 1ST, 1898.   NO. I

OUTPUT FOR 1898 $40,000,000.

FROM N° 8 EL DORADO.
PROPERTY OF CHAS. LAMB.
VALUE $ 315⁰⁰

DISCOVERER.
GEO. W. CARMACK.

THE LARGEST GOLD NUGGET.

An 1898 issue of the *Klondike News* claims strikes worth $40 million ($1 billion today) The Klondike was the site of the last great gold rush.

Conclusion

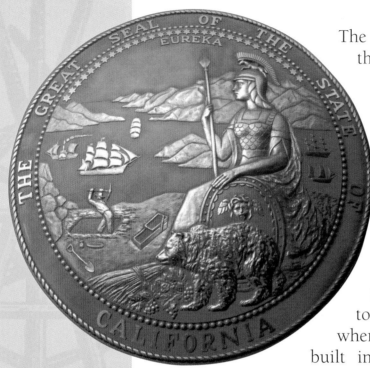

California's state seal is full of history: the bear of the Republic, the miner with his pick, the busy Sacramento River, the Sierra Nevada mountains, and the word *eureka* all remind people of the past. In the foreground, Minerva, the Roman goddess of wisdom, has grapes at her feet to represent the agricultural riches of the region.

The **seal** of the state of California bears the word *eureka*, a Greek word meaning "I have found it." This Greek word was placed on the state seal as a reminder of how important Marshall's discovery of gold was to California, the state now known as the "Golden State."

Sutter's Mill Today

California still celebrates its Gold Rush era. People can visit the site of Sutter's Mill and see a full-scale, historically accurate copy of the sawmill where Marshall found gold. The replica, built in 1968, is the centerpiece of the Marshall Gold Discovery State Historic Park.

In the early days of the Gold Rush, Coloma was a rowdy mining town with more than six thousand inhabitants and over a dozen hotels. Today, Coloma is a small, quiet community with about two hundred full-time residents. Most of Coloma is within the boundaries of the historic park.

The Mining Camps

Although Coloma has shrunk since Gold Rush days, California has grown spectacularly. Today it is one of the nation's richest, most populous states, with about 35 million residents.

Of the 546 different mining camps started in the Gold Rush, fewer than half survive today. Some, like Coloma, developed into towns or other reasonably sized communities. Others are still there, but as ghost towns. In most cases, however, only their curious names—such as French Corral, Brandy Flat, Scotch Hill, Soggsville, and Rough and Ready—remain as colorful reminders of California's past.

The Legacy of the California Gold Rush

The Gold Rush greatly speeded up the settlement of California. It also quickened the settlement of other new areas of the West. Thus the Gold Rush was an important factor in helping the nation realize its dream of Manifest Destiny.

The Gold Rush has also contributed to the great diversity in the state's heritage. Coming on the heels of Spanish and then Mexican occupation, the American settlers of the Gold Rush era never managed to eradicate those earlier influences from the rich and mixed culture of California. And the gold discovery brought with it a significant new influence—that of the Asian community that flourishes in California and elsewhere in the United States today.

The Gold Rush has left another, more negative legacy. Between 1850 and 1900, the gold mining industry used many millions of pounds of highly poisonous mercury to extract gold from rock and gravel. Much of that mercury is still contaminating lakes, rivers, and soil in California.

The ghost town of Bodie, California, has been preserved in a state of semi-decay. Visitors can walk around and imagine the town when it was bursting with forty-niners and bustling with activity.

43

Time Line

1542	Juan Rodríguez Cabrillo visits California.
1602	Sebastian Vizcaíno sails along California coast.
1769	First of California missions is founded.
1812	Russians establish Fort Ross.
1821	Republic of Mexico is established and Spanish rule of California ends.
1826	Jebediah Smith visits California.
1839	Johann Augustus Sutter founds Sutter's Fort.
1841	Russians sell Fort Ross to Sutter.
	First wagon train bringing American settlers arrives in California.
1845	United States offers to buy California from Mexico.
1846	May 13: Mexican War begins.
	June 10: Americans declare an independent Republic of California.
	July 9: United States claims California.
1848	January 24: James W. Marshall discovers gold at Sutter's Mill.
	February 2: Treaty of Guadalupe Hidalgo officially ends Mexican War. California becomes a U.S. possession.
	March 15: *Californian* newspaper publishes story on gold discovery.
	June: Second significant discovery of gold occurs near Coloma.
	August 17: Colonel Richard B. Mason publishes report on the gold strike.
	December 5: President Polk's message to Congress confirms discovery of large amounts of gold.
1849	February 28: First shipload of gold seekers arrives in San Francisco.
1859	Ninety thousand people come to California.
1850	California becomes thirty-first state.
1852	Foreign Miners' License Tax is passed in California legislature.
1854	Sacramento becomes capital of California.
1856	End of California Gold Rush.
1858	Gold and silver are discovered in Colorado near Pike's Peak.
1859	Comstock Lode is discovered in Nevada.
1860	California's population reaches 380,000.
1867	United States purchases Alaska from Russia.
1874	Gold is reported in Black Hills, South Dakota.
1896	Gold strike in Klondike region of Alaska.
1959	Alaska becomes forty-ninth state.

Glossary

census: official population count.

colony: settlement, area, or country owned or controlled by another nation.

currency: money or anything else used as a unit of exchange in a particular country.

deposit: natural accumulation in the ground of a substance.

frontier: edge of known or settled land. The frontier moved west across North America as white settlement expanded west onto new lands.

hydraulic: powered by a fluid, in this case water.

immigration: process of coming to a new country or region and taking up residence.

lease: arrange to use property of another person. An agreement made for this purpose is called a lease.

legislature: group of officials that makes laws.

lode: deposit of mineral in rock that contains valuable material, such as gold.

manifest: obviously true and easily recognizable. When white Americans used the phrase "Manifest Destiny," they meant it was obviously their destiny to expand the United States to the Pacific Ocean.

migration: movement of animals or people from one place to another.

mission: center built to establish Spanish settlement and convert Native Americans to Christianity. Missions in California also served to exploit the labor of Native peoples.

natural resources: naturally occurring materials—such as wood, oil, and gold—that can be used or sold, or amenities such as a good harbor or climate.

prospector: person who explores an area looking for mineral resources.

province: district of a nation that usually has its own capital town and some form of local government, similar to states in the United States.

republic: nation that has no sovereign or other unelected ruler, but is led by a leader or group of officials elected by its citizens.

sawmill: device for sawing logs.

seal: stamp bearing an official symbol.

shaft: vertical opening going down into the earth at a mining site.

strike: discovery of gold or other precious metal.

trapper: hunter who uses traps to kill animals such as beaver or squirrel for their fur.

treaty: agreement made between two or more people or groups of people after negotiation, usually at the end of a period of conflict.

United States Territory: geographical area that belongs to and is governed by the United States but is not included in any of its states.

Further Information

Books

Brimner, Larry Dane. *Angel Island* (Cornerstones of Freedom). Children's Press, 2001.

Green, Carl R. *The California Trail to Gold* (In American History). Enslow, 2000.

Gregory, Kristiana. *Seeds of Hope: The Gold Rush Diary of Susanna Fairchild* (Dear America). Scholastic, 2001.

Ingram, Scott. *California, the Golden State* (World Almanac Library of the States). World Almanac Library, 2002.

Press, Petra. *Indians of the Northwest: Traditions, History, Legends, and Life* (The Native Americans). Gareth Stevens, 2001.

Werther, Scott P. *The Donner Party* (Survivor). Children's Press, 2002.

Web Sites

www.californiahistoricalsociety.org California Historical Society web site has good information about all of California's history, including the Gold Rush.

www.library.ca.gov/goldrush/ California State Library offers excellent online exhibition all about the Gold Rush, including images and original documents.

www.parks.ca.gov/parkindex Index of the California State Park web site will take you to web pages about the following state historic parks: Marshall Gold Discovery, Sutter's Fort, and Fort Ross.

Useful Addresses

Marshall Gold Discovery State Historic Park
310 Back Street
Coloma, CA 95613
Telephone: (530) 622-3470

Index

Page numbers in *italics* indicate maps and diagrams. Page numbers in **bold** indicate other illustrations.